the *Beautiful* wife

Prayer Journal

Sandy Ralya

Kregel *Publications*

How to Use This Journal

*I*f you're anything like me, you want a great marriage but you aren't always willing to take the steps and do the hard work needed to produce the beautiful results you desire. You want fruit without pruning, perfume without petal-crushing, fitness without sweat . . . you get the picture. But maybe, just maybe, you have reached a point where you're craving more and are willing to try something new in order to experience different results. I came to that point over twenty years ago.

When my marriage was in trouble, I walked into church each Sunday morning desperate for help, but not daring to ask for it because everyone else's marriage seemed so perfect. My life appeared beautiful on the outside, but on the inside it was a mess.

Over time, I turned to God by reading the Bible and praying. I began candidly sharing about my problems with trusted friends, godly mentors, and wise Christian counselors, seeking their guidance. What I learned during that time transformed my life, and then God did an amazing work in my marriage. The loving support that I received from other women on my journey inspired me to become the founder and director of Beautiful Womanhood, a Christian mentoring ministry for wives. Beautiful Womanhood began in 2003 in Grand Rapids, Michigan, when I held the first Beautiful Womanhood seminar. I shared my personal testimony of how mentoring strengthened me—and eventually strengthened my marriage. Since then, I have shared my testimony at many events every year, and women around the world have participated in Beautiful Womanhood small groups.

The Beautiful Wife Prayer Journal is a place to chronicle all you will learn on your journey through *The Beautiful Wife*. In each chapter of this prayer journal, you will find prayers for you, your husband, and your marriage.

Space is also provided for you to journal your response to reflection questions and Scriptures that will deepen your understanding of God's Word as it relates to you and your marriage.

If you are attending a Beautiful Womanhood small group where *The Beautiful Wife* is being read and discussed, you are not at all obligated to use *The Beautiful Wife Prayer Journal*. But if you choose to use it, it will deepen your personal understanding of the material and enrich your knowledge of all that God desires to reveal to you about His wonderful plans for you and your marriage.

Each chapter in this journal should be completed after reading the corresponding chapter in *The Beautiful Wife*. For example, after reading chapter 1 in *The Beautiful Wife*, you would complete chapter 1 in *The Beautiful Wife Prayer Journal*, and so on. In some cases, you'll just begin a response, and then add to it as the weeks go by, such as page 8, where you will list your husband's prayer requests, or page 16, where you will list verses through which God is speaking to you. Your journal entries should be made during a time of quiet reflection at home, before meeting with your Beautiful Womanhood small group. Sharing from this journal is not mandatory for group participation. You may choose to take your journal along, in case you feel led to share an entry with the group, or you may use it solely for personal introspection.

- Pray the prayer found in the beginning of each chapter. Journal any inspiration or challenges this prayer evokes.
- Journal honestly and prayerfully in response to each question. Remember that sharing what you write with the group is not mandatory. What you write here is primarily for your own benefit.
- Construct a response to the Scripture verses listed for each chapter. When journaling your responses, ask yourself if you are following the Bible's instruction and, if not, why? Make a list of small steps you could take to obey God's Word and experience better results in your life and marriage.
- Fashion the listed Scripture verses into prayers. Personalize the passages for greater impact. When you lack the strength or creativity to voice your own prayers, it's a blessing to borrow from Scripture.

So many passages in the Bible can be used to pray for yourself, your husband, and your marriage. (Examples are included with each chapter.) God honors His Word and causes it to accomplish all He wants! His Word always produces fruit (Isaiah 55:11).

That said, it's important to note that taking Scripture out of context or citing verses for selfish purposes is a bad idea and won't profit you. Instead, focus on forming prayers from Scripture that edify your spirit, instruct you in the things of God, and benefit your husband. When gathering applicable verses, an easy online resource for looking up a key word or searching for a specific topic is www.biblegateway.com.

- Record prayer requests for your life and marriage that are related to the topic of each chapter. Make sure to come back to these pages and record how and when these prayers are answered. Rereading answers to prayer will increase your faith in God.
- Keep reviewing and rereading your journal entries! Doing so heightens an understanding of your weaknesses and need for God, and prevents a lot of aimless wandering and confusion. As you fill it with honest reflections, this journal will become a go-to source of personal marital wisdom.
- After chronicling your journey through all twelve chapters, refer back to this journal throughout the life of your marriage. Take time to recognize and be encouraged by God's faithfulness when you consider how far He has brought you. As you read and reread your responses, I pray you will be inspired to see yourself in a new light, or will be motivated to take new steps in a different direction than you've been heading.

When desiring better results in your life and marriage, it's important to take new steps—such as journaling. Change isn't easy, but it's worth any effort you invest. Whether you're working through this prayer journal on your own, or using it in addition to your discussion within a Beautiful Womanhood small group, I believe you'll find loving encouragement to go the distance with your husband. Motivate yourself to make this investment by picturing the deeper intimacy with God and your husband you would like to experience. As you invest precious time journaling and praying, expect to receive fresh insights about what it means to be a beautiful wife, and God-given answers to your prayers.

You'll experience a rite of passage within this prayer journal that will mark your progress as you journey toward becoming a beautiful wife who is focused on God and is experiencing greater fulfillment in her marriage. May the Holy Spirit's power fill you and work through you to fulfill all the plans God has for you and your marriage. Let's begin!

CHAPTER ONE

Equipping for the Journey

Pray this prayer every day for at least one week, inserting your husband's name in the blank. Journal your daily reflections below.

Dear God, thank You for _____. Help me to see him the way You do. Encourage my husband to love You with all his heart, soul, mind, and strength. Remind me to turn to You first when I don't know what to do. Help me to worship You as I should. As I read the Bible and pray, help me to understand my role as a wife. Fill me with patience as I wait for Your guidance and answers to my prayers. Please give me the courage to share openly and honestly with the women who surround me so I can be strengthened with love, purpose, and hope. In Jesus' name, amen.

Day 1

Day 2

Day 3

Day 4

Day 5

Day 6

Day 7

List your husband's prayer requests, and pray for them regularly. When they are answered, record how and when.

My Husband's Prayer Requests	*Answers to Prayer*

List your prayer requests for your husband, and pray for them regularly. Keep a record of God's answers.

My Prayers for My Husband	Answers to Prayer
His strengths used for God's glory	
His weaknesses strengthened/healed	
Godly friends who will encourage spiritual growth	
Emotional safety/healing	
Physical safety/healing	

Write down any prayer requests you may have. In particular, do you have any prayer requests related to turning to God, understanding your role as wife, and sharing within a community of women? Remember to come back and note each answer to these prayers.

My Prayer Requests	*Answers to Prayer*

Memorize Psalm 119:35. Journal your response.

Put in writing your response to God's Word when thinking about yourself and your marriage.

Titus 2:3–5

Mark 11:24–25

Philippians 4:6–7

Genesis 2:18

Ecclesiastes 4:9–10

Over the next few weeks, list Scripture verses that describe God's attributes. Begin with the letter "a" and move through the alphabet. Reading and re-reading these verses will cause your trust in Him to grow. Add to this list as you discover more about our wonderful God. Form each verse into a prayer of praise by using the following illustration as a guide.

A **Amazing** (1 Chronicles 16:24): Lord, You perform glorious deeds among the nations. I will tell everyone about the amazing things You do!

B **Blessing-Giver** (Ephesians 1:3): I praise God, the Father of our Lord Jesus Christ, who has blessed me with every spiritual blessing in the heavenly realms because I belong to Christ.

C

D

E

F

G

H

I

J

K

L

M

N

O

P

Q

R

S

T

U

V

W

X

Y

Z

List verses to pray for your husband; insert his name where appropriate.

Example: Psalm 1:2— May _____ delight in doing everything You want, Lord; day and night may he think about Your law.

List verses of encouragement through which God speaks to you; personalize them where appropriate.

Example: Colossians 3:16—Let the words of Christ, in all their richness, live in my heart and make me wise.

CHAPTER TWO

Attending to Self-Care

Pray this prayer every day for at least one week. Journal any thoughts or inspiration that come to mind.

Dear Jesus, daily remind me that there is really only one thing worth being concerned about—spending quiet moments with you. Guard and guide me as I tackle the source of unhealthy emotions. Lead me to the help I need to deal with emotions that plague me. Help me take control of my wild thought life so I can experience Your peace, and help me to control my tongue and cause good things to come from the words I say. Direct my path as I take care of myself and my marriage by eating better, moving more, and getting enough rest. Amen.

Day 1

Day 2

Day 3

Day 4

Day 5

Day 6

Day 7

Spend quiet time with God each day. Meditate on one thought from His Word. Record each day's thought and your response here.

Day 1

Day 2

Day 3

Day 4

Day 5

Day 6

Day 7

As God gives you more verses of encouragement, add to your list on page 16.

What can you do to ensure regular spiritual self-care? Write out your plan.

Are you experiencing any of the following emotions: guilt, shame, envy, anger, sadness, or fear? If so . . .

+ What is your response to this emotion? Do you escape into books, television, Internet, or busyness? Do you medicate with shopping, activity, food, or alcohol? List your responses.

+ Can you remember the source or cause of this emotion? If so, record it here. If not, ask God to reveal it.

+ When you're feeling this emotion, what do you tell yourself? Write your response.

+ Does what you are telling yourself line up with God's Word? If not, what does God's Word say about it?

Record any healthy eating suggestions you are willing to implement in your life. Write down any unhealthy foods you will begin eliminating from your diet.

Write a prayer asking God to help you find time and motivation to care for your body by exercising.

How is a stressful schedule impacting your marriage? What one activity will you eliminate?

Make a list of small, peaceful, pleasurable activities that refresh you. Which one(s) could become a regular part of each day? Journal about how you will make time to fit them into your schedule.

Journal your response to God's Word about how to practice self-care.

Philippians 4:8

Proverbs 14:30

Matthew 11:28

Proverbs 22:3

Genesis 1:29

Mark 2:27

Rewrite Psalm 119:80 in your own words. Journal a prayer of response.

Prayer Requests for "Attending to Self-Care"	*Answers to Prayer*

CHAPTER THREE

Living as the Genuine Article

Pray this prayer every day for at least one week. Journal any thoughts that the Holy Spirit inspires.

Dear Jesus, help me realize which masks I wear and why I wear them. In the light and safety of Your love, encourage me to lower these masks and ultimately remove them. Help me remember that living without masks is necessary if I'm going to connect with and offer hope to others who are struggling. Heal the real me behind the mask. I ask in Jesus' name. Amen.

Day 1

Day 2

Day 3

Day 4

Day 5

Day 6

Day 7

Journal about the mask you wear (Superwoman, Material Girl, Perfect Ten, etc.) and why you've worn it.

Journal your thoughts and feelings about telling someone close to you about your mask, and about lowering it to show the real you.

Talk with your husband about the type of mask you've worn and why you've worn it. Ask him how, if in any way, it's affected your marriage. Record his response and your reaction.

Journal a response to God's Word about throwing away your mask and living as the genuine article.

Romans 11:6

Matthew 6:19–21

Examine your life in the light of Colossians 3:12 (MSG) written out for you below. Journal a prayer of response.

So, chosen by God for this new life of love, dress in the wardrobe God picked out for you: compassion, kindness, humility, quiet strength, discipline. Be even-tempered, content with second place, quick to forgive an offense. Forgive as quickly and completely as the Master forgave you. And regardless of what else you put on, wear love. It's your basic, all-purpose garment. Never be without it.

"Living as the Genuine Article" Prayer Requests   **Answers to Prayer**

CHAPTER FOUR

Cultivating Mystique

Pray this prayer every day for at least one week. Record any thoughts or inspiration that come to mind.

Lord, help me understand the depth of Your love for me. Replace the lies of the enemy with the truth of Your Word. Work out Your plans for my life. Show me where I can take steps to fulfill Your plans for me. Help me show love for my husband by taking care of my appearance. Finally, help me walk in encouragement, discretion, and courage so I can be a blessing to my husband and all those around me. Amen.

Day 1

Day 2

Day 3

Day 4

Day 5

Day 6

Day 7

Keep a running list of verses that describe how God feels about you, along with a summary of the verse in your own words. Here are a few to get you started:

I am loved by God. (Ephesians 2:4)

Nothing can separate me from His love. (Romans 8:38)

He chose me. (Ephesians 1:4)

God bought me at a high price. (1 Corinthians 6:20)

I am His masterpiece. (Ephesians 2:10)

I can be victorious through Christ who loves me. (Romans 8:37)

God's mighty power works within me to accomplish more than I could ask, think, hope, or imagine. (Ephesians 3:20)

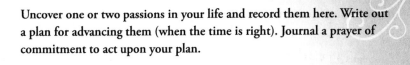

Uncover one or two passions in your life and record them here. Write out a plan for advancing them (when the time is right). Journal a prayer of commitment to act upon your plan.

Write out Ephesians 2:10, inserting your name into the passage.

Journal your response to God's Word as you reflect on the different aspects of cultivating mystique.

Ephesians 3:17–19

Romans 12:2

Psalm 138:8

Luke 10:38–42

Proverbs 11:20

Proverbs 11:25

Start a running list of verses containing promises God gives in His Word. When your husband needs encouragement, come back to these pages and use these verses to refresh him in prayer.

Example: Proverbs 3:3—Never let loyalty and kindness get away from
_____. May he wear them like a necklace; may they be written deep within his heart. Then _____ will find favor with both God and people and he will gain a good reputation.

Prayer Requests as I "Cultivate Mystique"	Answers to Prayer

CHAPTER FIVE

Inviting Romance

Pray this prayer every day for at least one week. Journal your daily responses below.

Lord, help me mark out a new path for my feet—one that invites my husband to romance. I relinquish my control issues to You, knowing that You watch over me and care about what happens to me. Help me fulfill my part of the contract to take refuge in You, assured by Your words that You will be my protector. Committing myself to obey Your Word, I will respect my husband. Remind me to focus on my husband's positive attributes, as I would like him to do for me. Help me to seek Your wisdom and build my house by conveying confidence to my husband that he can do everything with the help of Christ who strengthens him. Amen.

Day 1

Day 2

Day 3

Day 4

Day 5

Day 6

Day 7

Prayerfully consider which area(s) of TRACE you need to work on improving. Record them here.

> **T**RUST instead of control
> **R**ESPECT instead of demean
> **A**PPRECIATE instead of
>   criticize
> **C**ONFER CONFIDENCE
>   instead of doubt
> **E**XPOSE VULNERABILITY
>   instead of defensiveness

Share the five TRACE steps with your husband. Ask him to name one or two of your bad habits that inhibit the romance he feels toward you. Write what he says here and journal your reaction.

List your husband's positive traits and actions. How could you show appreciation for him now and in the following weeks? After doing so, come back and record his response.

Positive Traits/Actions	My Appreciation	His Response

Put in writing your response to God's Word when thinking about inviting romance.

Genesis 3:16

Philippians 2:3

1 Peter 5:7

Ephesians 5:33

Philippians 4:8

Proverbs 14:1

Romans 8:6

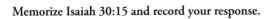

Memorize Isaiah 30:15 and record your response.

What are your defensiveness triggers? What underlying factors motivate your defensiveness?

Prayer Requests as I "Invite Romance"	Answers to Prayer

CHAPTER SIX

Thinking Differently About Sex

Pray this prayer every day for at least one week. Journal any thoughts that the Holy Spirit inspires.

Lord, transform me into a new person by changing the way I think about sex. Help me to fully understand all that the sexual relationship provides as You designed it. Heal me where sexual wounds have been inflicted, emotionally and physically. Set me free from the past so I can partake of the future with joy. Forgive me for the times I withheld this gift from my husband when it was within my power to give. Help me to see myself as You see me: desirable. May this gift of sex ignite a new awareness in me of Your pursuit to embrace me at the core of my being with a love beyond that of any man. Amen.

Day 1

Day 2

Day 3

Day 4

Day 5

Day 6

Day 7

Journal about any anger, sorrow, pain, or hurt you endure(d) as a result of past or present negative sexual experiences. Lament your losses as David did in the Psalms. (For example, Psalm 22:1: "My God, my God, why have you abandoned me? Why are you so far away when I groan for help?") God's comfort begins when you trust enough to open up and put words to the flood of questions, emotions, and painful memories. God wants you to cry out to Him. He will hear and He will answer.

Journal your response to any revelations discovered in "What Does Your Husband Think About Sex?" (*The Beautiful Wife,* p. 112).

Talk with your husband about your sexual relationship. Allow him the opportunity to share his feelings; carefully listen to all he says. Journal a response.

Devise a plan with changes you can make (based on your husband's input above) with God's and possibly other people's help, to recapture this vital part of your marriage. Record your plan here.

Journal a response to God's Word concerning sex.

Genesis 2:22–25

Matthew 19:5–6

1 Corinthians 6:18–20

1 Corinthians 7:3–4

1 Corinthians 7:2, 5

1 Corinthians 7:34

> *For many people, sex is the most tangible experience they know of feeling loved and wanted by another person.*
> —*Paula Rinehart,* Sex and the Soul of a Woman

God uses the experience of sex to help you comprehend a greater mystery: that He pursues you until you and He are one. The apostle Paul says, "This is a great mystery, but is an illustration of the way Christ and the church are united into one" (Ephesians 5:32). Journal a prayer of response.

Prayer Requests for "Thinking Differently About Sex"	Answers to Prayer

CHAPTER SEVEN

Opening Lines of Communication

Pray this prayer every day for at least one week. Journal any thoughts or inspiration that come to mind.

Dear Lord, please help me as I practice effective communication skills. Show me where I've lacked understanding toward my husband. Grow in me the fruit of the Spirit—love, joy, peace, patience, kindness, goodness, faithfulness, gentleness, and self-control—so I can be a tool of grace extended toward my husband. Guide me as I seek to open lines of communication in my marriage. Amen.

Day 1

Day 2

Day 3

Day 4

Day 5

Day 6

Day 7

Evaluate your listening skills, direct communication, and kindness. What area needs improvement? Open your heart to what God has to say, and repent for anything He reveals. What will you commit to do to improve?

Have you ever chosen an improper time and/or place to communicate something to your husband? What was the result? Ask your husband for forgiveness and journal his response.

Journal your response to God's Word about opening the lines of communication.

James 1:19

Isaiah 55:3

James 3:2

Instead of telling your husband about your day, choose three specific questions to ask in the course of an evening that will draw him into conversation about his day. Be sure that they're not questions that can be answered with one word. When he answers, practice mirroring, validating, and empathizing. Afterward, journal about each phase of the discussion. How did it go? What can you do better next time?

Initiate an open, honest discussion with your husband about the communication within your marriage. Begin the conversation with the words, "I'd like your input," *not* "We need to talk!" Use the communication techniques discussed in the chapter: be direct and kind, choose the proper place and time, and listen to understand. Record your experience here.

The book of Proverbs is full of wisdom on many topics, but it is especially filled with wise advice about communication. Read one chapter of Proverbs every day for the next month. (We'll read Proverbs 31 later.) Journal the insights you gain here.

1

2

3

4

5

6

7

8

9

10

11

12

13

14

15

16

17

18

19

20

21

22

23

24

25

26

27

28

29

30

Journal a prayer of response to Proverbs 19:14.

Prayer Requests for "Open Communication"	*Answers to Prayer*

CHAPTER EIGHT

Speaking Truth in Love

Pray this prayer every day for at least one week. Journal any thoughts or ideas the Holy Spirit inspires.

Lord, I pray that I will become more like You by learning to speak the truth in love. May I learn to distinguish between sin and annoyances. Help me examine my life in the light of Your Word to determine whether I'm responding to my husband with sin, and, if so, give me the courage I need to make changes. I want to receive all the love You have for me so that I can love my husband with a love that overcomes sin and conquers evil. Help me forgive him when he hurts me— keeping no lists. Give me wisdom to use words that will bring healing, speaking respectfully, honestly, and patiently. Amen.

Day 1

Day 2

Day 3

Day 4

Day 5

Day 6

Day 7

What difficult issue are you facing that would benefit from you speaking truth in love? If you aren't currently facing a difficult issue in your marriage, is there another relationship or situation you've encountered that would benefit from this principle?

+ Examine your own actions within the struggle to speak truth in love, and record any conflict between your actions and Scripture (as I did on pages 144–45, *The Beautiful Wife*).

- Fill in the blanks: I feel _____

  when you _____ .

- Read 1 Corinthians 13:4–7 and record a prayer of response in light of the sinful issue you face.

> *Go back to page 35 and add to your list of your husband's positive traits and actions. How can you affirm those and encourage him this week?*

Journal a response to God's Word concerning speaking truth in love.

John 8:31–32

Ephesians 5:13–14

James 1:5

1 John 4:19

Luke 6:37–38

Continue journaling a response to God's Word concerning speaking truth in love.

2 Timothy 1:7

1 Peter 4:8

Proverbs 12:18

John 15:5

Do you have more attributes of God to add to the list on pages 12–15? If so, do so now.

Prayer Requests for "Speaking Truth in Love"	Answers to Prayer

CHAPTER NINE

Managing Money

Pray this prayer every day for at least one week. Journal any thoughts that the Holy Spirit inspires.

Lord, thank You for the money and possessions You've entrusted to me. They are gifts, and I'm grateful. I confess all the wrong thoughts and attitudes about money that I've carried with me into marriage, like . . .

Change me! Please bring me and my husband into unity about tithing, because I want to take Your challenge and see You provide for our needs with 90 percent as we give You 10 percent. Help us to see beyond this materialistic culture so we can reach those who don't have as much as we do. Give us wisdom as we devise a plan for our finances. Bring us closer together as we implement this plan. Amen.

Day 1

Day 2

Day 3

Day 4

Day 5

Day 6

Day 7

Write down your thoughts about money that were formed in your past. How have they affected your marriage? Pray that God will change any faulty thinking and replace it with right thinking.

Write down your thoughts about God's ownership of your finances.

Journal your response to God's Word about managing money.

Malachi 3:10

Proverbs 3:9

2 Corinthians 8:13–14

Philippians 4:11

1 Timothy 6:6, 8

Keep a running list of verses you find about money. Read them regularly to increase your knowledge of wise money management and to free you from wrong thinking about money.

Example: 1 Timothy 6:10—"For the love of money is at the root of all kinds of evil. And some people, craving money, have wandered from the faith and pierced themselves with many sorrows."

Have you and your husband created a plan for your finances? How has this plan—or lack of a plan—affected your marriage? What changes do you personally need to make for your finances—and your marriage—to improve? Ask for God's guidance and help.

"Managing Money" Prayer Requests	*Answers to Prayer*

CHAPTER TEN

Creating a Culture of Beauty

Pray this prayer every day for at least one week. Journal any thoughts that the Holy Spirit inspires.

Dear Lord, I desire to create a home that is a shelter from life's storms. Thank You for giving me a home in which I can express beauty. Show me the negative attitudes I have that tear my house down, and help me replace them with peace and contentment. Reveal to me where I can change my priorities to focus better on my marriage. Help me to open my home to those needing refuge. Amen.

Day 1

Day 2

Day 3

Day 4

Day 5

Day 6

Day 7

Journal a prayer asking God to lead you in expressing your unique personality or style in your home in a way that would bring honor to Him. Ask Him to give you creative ideas for expressing beauty, and skill in communicating those ideas to your husband. Revisit this prayer every day this week, and journal how you sense God directing.

Jot down words that define your personal style along with creative ways to express beauty in your home. Be prepared to start small and compromise when necessary. Share your plan for expressing your personal style at home with your husband. (If you meet with resistance, come back and journal your frustration, knowing God cares about you and the details of your life. Remind yourself that the most important aspect of a beautiful home is the people living there.)

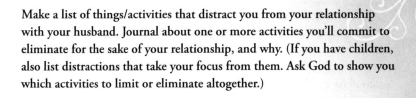

Make a list of things/activities that distract you from your relationship with your husband. Journal about one or more activities you'll commit to eliminate for the sake of your relationship, and why. (If you have children, also list distractions that take your focus from them. Ask God to show you which activities to limit or eliminate altogether.)

Journal about any negative attitudes that have plagued you. What godly attitudes should replace them? Ask your husband to pray for you as you begin replacing negative attitudes with godly ones.

What triggers cause the emotional barometer to rise in your home?

Refer back to page 35. Continue to add to the list of positive qualities you observe in your husband. Affirming those traits will create a culture of appreciation at home.

If you do not regularly sit down to eat as a family, make a list of any obstacles preventing family dinnertime along with solutions for how to remove or overcome them. If you do regularly eat as a family, is the time pleasant or confrontational? Enriching or unraveling? What steps can you take to make mealtime a more positive experience?

Prayerfully make a list of people who might benefit from spending time in your home. Plan now to invite them one by one.

Journal your response to God's Word about expressing beauty in and through your home.

Psalm 19:1

James 3:5

Proverbs 27:15–16

1 Peter 3:1–2

Proverbs 21:19

Philippians 4:11

Rewrite Proverbs 31:27 in your own words, and journal a prayer of response to it.

Prayer Requests as I "Create a Culture of Beauty"	Answers to Prayer

CHAPTER ELEVEN

Professionalizing the Roles of Wife and Mother

Pray this prayer every day for at least one week, longer if needed. Journal any thoughts or plans the Holy Spirit inspires.

Dear Lord, remind me to talk to You about my marriage, before talking to anyone. Help me to listen to Your instruction concerning my role as a wife. Use others to encourage me to focus my attention on my actions rather than my husband's. I ask for Your help in determining a vision for my role as a wife for the benefit of my marriage, and for the creativity to devise a plan of action to carry out the inspiration You've placed in my heart. Create in me and my husband a strong desire for unity in all aspects of our marriage—including children. Increase my eagerness to learn everything You want to teach me about my roles of wife and mother. In Jesus' name, amen.

Day 1

Day 2

Day 3

Day 4

Day 5

Day 6

Day 7

Record a prayer request concerning a weakness in your life that needs strengthening for the sake of your husband and/or children. Also pray that God will reveal your strengths and how He might use them for the benefit of your husband and/or children. These may provide clues that will help you determine the vision God desires you to fulfill in your marriage.

With God's help, determine a vision for your role as a wife and record it here. Develop and journal a plan of action for that vision that will lead to its fulfillment.

List any Bible passages that God used in helping you determine a vision for your role as a wife. List other Scripture verses that will encourage you to persevere.

If you have children, prayerfully determine a vision for your children and record it here. Develop and journal a plan of action for that vision that will lead to its fulfillment. If you do not have children, journal your expectations for the future in relation to children.

If you have children, list any Bible passages that God used in helping you determine a vision for them. List other Scripture verses that you can share with your children as you pursue this vision. If you do not have children, journal a prayer, surrendering yourself to God's plan for your future in relation to children.

Mark your calendar for a year from today. On that day, revisit these plans and see what progress you have made. As your marriage evolves and children grow, plans may need to be periodically updated to reflect new circumstances.

Journal a response to God's Word concerning marriage and motherhood.

Psalm 133

1 Peter 5:8

Titus 2:4

Read Proverbs 31 and list the attributes and character traits this wife and mother possesses. In areas where you see your personal weakness compared to her, journal a prayer of response. (Most commentators believe that this is a composite of the ideal woman rather than an actual woman, so don't despair!)

Prayer Requests for my "Roles of Wife and Mother"	Answers to Prayer

CHAPTER TWELVE

Choosing God's Best

Pray this prayer every day for at least one week. Journal any thoughts or decisions the Holy Spirit inspires.

Jesus, shut my ears to the culture's influence that says I can have it all. Increase my awareness of this lie and the effect it has on my choices. I admit that I can't grow my marriage on my own. I need Your help! Help me choose Your best by allowing You to govern the choices I make as a wife. Lead me, for I put my hope in You. Amen.

Day 1

Day 2

Day 3

Day 4

Day 5

Day 6

Day 7

Journal your reflections about what ways you have tried to "have it all" and how this has affected your marriage.

Journal about the area of your marriage that needs the most attention. Review the chapter that deals with that area, and list the steps you are going to take to choose God's best.

Journal a response to God's Word about choosing God's best.

Psalm 25:4–5

Psalm 25:9–10

Journal a prayer of response to Deuteronomy 30:19. In this prayer, repent of choices that have brought death rather than life to your marriage. Also record your acknowledgment of God's forgiveness.

"Choosing God's Best" Prayer Requests	*Answers to Prayer*

Keep writing in this journal and reviewing what you have written! Doing so sharpens an understanding of your weaknesses and need for God. As you chronicle all you learn and observe God's faithfulness, you will appreciate how far He has brought you. Refer to this journal as an ongoing source of personal marital wisdom. Blessings, Sandy